AMERICAN LEGENDS™

Jim Bowie

Marianne Johnston

The Rosen Publishing Group's

PowerKids Press™

New York

Published in 2001 by The Rosen Publishing Group, Inc.
29 East 21st Street, New York, NY 10010

First Edition

Book Design: Michael de Guzman

Photo Credits: p. 4 by Debra Wainwright; pp. 8, 11, 12, 15, 16, 20 © North Wind Pictures; p. 7 © John Terrence Turner/FPG International; p. 19 © Lowell Georgia/CORBIS.

Johnston, Marianne.
      Jim Bowie / Marianne Johnston.
         p. cm.— (American legends)
      Includes index.
      Summary: This book introduces Jim Bowie, describing his early life on the frontier, his fighting skills, and his part in the Texas Revolution.
      ISBN 0-8239-5578-8
      1. Bowie, James, d. 1836—Juvenile literature. 2. Pioneers—Texas—Biography—Juvenile literature. [1. Bowie, James, d. 1836. 2. Pioneers.] I. Title. II. Series.
      2000
      976.4'03'092—dc21
      [B]

Manufactured in the United States of America

Contents

Jim Bowie was six feet tall. He had fair skin and reddish-brown hair. He was a strong fighter and learned how to ride wild alligators when he was a boy.

Jim Bowie

There once was a man who knew no fear. He rode alligators through swamps and could beat anybody in a fight. In 1836, he was at the famous Battle of the Alamo in Texas. The man's name was James Bowie, but everybody called him Jim. Jim was six feet (1.8 m) tall. He was strong and had a solid build. He had reddish-brown hair and fair skin.

Much of the truth about Jim Bowie's life has been **exaggerated**, or made to be bigger or more important than it was. Over the years, wild stories were told about Jim's bravery in the wilderness and about his strength in fights. Jim Bowie became a **legend**.

What Is a Legend?

A legend is a story that has come down from the past. Sometimes a legend is about a person from an earlier time who is so interesting that many stories are told about that person. The stories may or may not be true. We like to make heroes out of these people because they had qualities we would like to have ourselves. Jim Bowie was strong and brave. We want to be strong and brave, too.

A **legendary** person might also have qualities we do not admire. Jim Bowie was this type of person, too. He was known as a powerful fighter who lived during the **frontier** days of the early 1800s. Back then being a good fighter meant that you were strong enough to survive.

We like to read or hear about legends. A large part of Jim Bowie's legend is about his being a good fighter. Today we admire people who know how to deal nicely with others. Heroes today get along with others who are different from them.

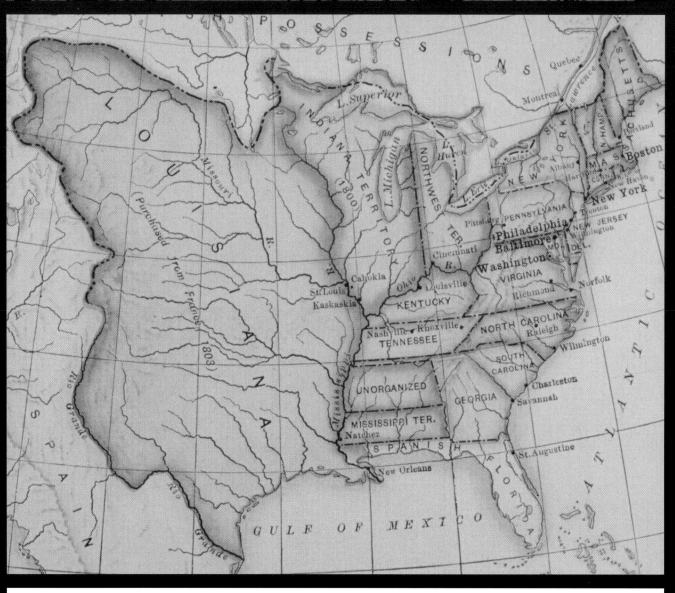

This map of 1803 shows the Louisiana Purchase. Jim and his family lived in the wilderness of Louisiana. Their home was surrounded by wild animals and plants. Much of the food the Bowies ate came from the wilderness around them.

A Childhood on the Move

Jim Bowie was born in Kentucky in the spring of 1796. He had two older brothers, three older sisters, and two younger brothers.

In those days, lots of **settlers** were moving to new lands west of the Mississippi River. In 1800, the Bowie family decided to move, too. At the age of four, little Jim began the first of many adventures in his life. The Bowie family moved a lot during the next nine years. They went from Kentucky to Missouri and then to Louisiana. Each home Jim lived in as a child was surrounded by wilderness. Settlers who lived on the frontier had to build their own homes and clear land for farming. Although life was hard, Jim learned to love the wilderness.

Riding an Alligator

Jim and his older brother Rezin were rowdy, or rough, as boys. Some of the neighbors called them the "wild Bowie boys." The brothers loved to explore the wilderness. The Bowie boys were not afraid of the bears that roamed the nearby forests and **prairies**. They were not scared of the alligators and snakes that lived in the **bayou** either. The boys liked to explore these swampy areas near the Bowie home in Louisiana.

Legend says that Jim started riding alligators when he was a boy. He would rope shut the huge jaws of dangerous alligators. Then he would jump on the alligators' backs and go for wild rides through the swamps!

Jim and his brother loved to roam the bayou near their home. It is said that Jim often roped alligators' jaws shut and rode on their backs through the bayou. As he got older, Jim would not even bother roping the jaws shut.

These hunters have captured a bear and are carrying it out of the woods. Jim was an excellent hunter and often tracked wild deer and bears.

Growing Up

Jim moved out of his family's home when he was 18 years old. He settled on land near his family. He used all the outdoor skills he had learned as a boy. He hunted wild deer, bears, and alligators.

During these years Jim was known as a fighter. Legend says he got into many fights. One fight, called the Sandbar Duel, might have been the start of many tales about Jim's fighting skills. He was about 31 years old. The fight took place along the river near Natchez, Mississippi. Many people were in the fight, including Jim. He was shot in his lung and thigh. He was also stabbed seven times. Somehow, Jim was able to survive. News of the fight and Jim's part in it spread across the country.

The Pirate Jean Laffite

In 1819, Jim met the **notorious** pirate Jean Laffite. This man was an **outlaw**. He led a dangerous life as a **smuggler**. Jim helped Laffite smuggle Africans into Louisiana. These Africans were then sold as slaves to work on **plantations**. Slavery was not against the law then, but bringing slaves into the country was.

Slavery was terrible and cruel. People want to forget that the real Jim Bowie took part in the slave business. That is probably why this fact about Jim's life is not a big part of his legend.

The famous pirate Jean Laffite is shown here sitting in a hammock.
Jim Bowie helped Laffite smuggle slaves into Louisiana.

Silver miners in Mexico in the 1860s. Jim spent most of 1830 looking for silver mines that he had been told about while living with the Lipan Apache, a Native American people. He never found the mines.

The Search for Lost Silver Mines

Jim moved to Texas in 1830, settling in San Antonio. Texas was not a part of the United States at that time. It belonged to Mexico. In Texas Jim heard stories of silver mines full of treasure. The mines were supposed to be somewhere to the northwest of San Antonio. Legend says Jim found several old treasure maps that he thought would lead him to these mines. He set out to find them with a group of men and mules. They traveled through the dry **chaparral** toward the San Saba River. The mines were thought to be located near the river. Jim never found the mines. Native Americans attacked Jim and the others. Jim was lucky to make it back to San Antonio alive.

The Texas Revolution

Jim became active in **politics**. In 1831, he married Ursula Veramendi. The following year, Jim led a group of Texas landowners against the Mexican government. They did not like the way the Mexican government was treating them. They wanted to be free from Mexican rule. A terrible illness called cholera began to spread throughout the area. In 1833, many people, including Jim's wife, died from the illness.

The Texas **Revolution** began in October 1835. Jim became an officer in the Texas army to help fight against Mexico. The most famous battle of the Texas Revolution was the Battle of the Alamo. Jim Bowie fought his last fight at the Alamo.

This monument honors the Texan soldiers, including Jim Bowie, who died at the Alamo. Today visitors can see the grounds and buildings of the Alamo. People now remember the battle as a heroic struggle against a much bigger army.

The Battle of the Alamo. Legend says that Jim slept on his bed with two guns and a knife. When the Mexican soldiers came in, he shot as many as he could. Most likely, though, he was too sick to raise his head when the enemy attacked.

The Battle of the Alamo

The Alamo was an old **mission** that was made into a fort near San Antonio. Jim and about 182 other Texan soldiers, including Davy Crockett, moved into the Alamo on February 23, 1836. They knew that the Mexican army would be coming to the Alamo soon.

Jim became sick with a disease known as typhoid at the Alamo. Typhoid causes a high fever and stomach problems and can lead to death. Even though he was sick and could not fight, Jim stayed at the Alamo to help the Texas army. On March 6, 1836, after a fierce and bloody fight, the Texans lost the battle against the Mexican army. Jim Bowie was killed in his bed.

Remembering Jim Bowie

The town of Menard, Texas, is very close to the area where Jim Bowie searched for the lost silver mines. Each year the people of Menard hold a festival called the Jim Bowie Days Celebration. Visitors enjoy storytelling, pony races, and games. People in the festival also act in a play about Jim Bowie. The play tells about one legend when Jim lived with the Lipan Apache, a Native American people. It is said that the chief of the Lipan told Jim about the lost silver mines near San Antonio.

People can visit the Jim Bowie House in Opelousas, Louisiana, to learn more about Jim's life. Today people can also go to the Alamo in San Antonio, Texas.

Glossary

bayou (BY-yoo) Marshy or swampy bodies of water in the southern United States.

chaparral (sha-pah-RAL) A dry landscape of shrubby plants found in parts of Texas.

exaggerated (ihg-zah-juh-RAY-ted) When a statement has been blown up to go beyond the truth to make it more interesting and entertaining.

frontier (frun-TEER) The edge of settled country, where the wilderness begins.

legend (LEH-jend) A story passed down through the years that many people believe.

legendary (LEH-jen-der-ee) To be famous and important.

mission (MIH-shun) A religious center that helps people in a community.

notorious (no-TOHR-ee-us) Someone who is famous, especially because he or she is bad.

outlaw (OWT-law) A person who does not obey the law.

plantations (plan-TAY-shuns) Large farms in the southern part of the United States where slaves were often used to do the work.

politics (POL-ih-tiks) Having to do with elections and governments.

prairies (PRAYR-ees) Large areas of flat land with grass but few or no trees.

revolution (REH-vuh-loo-shun) A complete change in government.

settlers (SEH-tuh-lers) People who move to a new land to live.

smuggler (SMUH-glur) A person who moves things in and out of a country in a way that is against the law.

Index

A
adventures, 9
alligators, 5, 10, 13

B
Battle of the Alamo,
    5, 18, 21
Bowie, Rezin, 10

C
cholera, 18
Crockett, Davy, 21

F
family, 9, 13
fight, 5, 13, 18, 21

frontier, 6, 9

H
heroes, 6

J
Jim Bowie Days
    Celebration, 22
Jim Bowie House, 22

L
Laffite, Jean, 14

N
Native American, 17,
    22

S
Sandbar Duel, 13
silver mines, 17, 22
slaves, 14

T
Texas Revolution, 18
typhoid, 21

V
Veramendi, Ursula,
    18

W
wilderness, 9, 10

Web Sites

To learn more about Jim Bowie, check out these Web sites:
http://www.tsha.utexas.edu/handbook/online/index.html (Type Jim Bowie
    into the search engine.)
http://www.menardtexas.com/sos.htm